More Aster(ix) Anthologies

Mothers Unearthed
September 2022

Winter Fiction
December 2021

Best of Hot Metal Bridge
April 2021

The Ferrante Project
October 2020

The Poetry Issue
Winter 2020

Inheritance
Summer 2019

(Un)bound [double issue]
Winter 2018/2019

as well as...

Edges - Fall 2018

Dirty Laundry - Fall 2017

Kitchen Table Translation - Summer 2017

and more!

available for order wherever books are sold

and don't forget to visit
asterixjournal.com
for more content and information

Aster(ix) Journal
www.asterixjournal.com

Editor-in-Chief/Founder
Angie Cruz

Publisher/Founder
Adriana E. Ramírez

Senior Editor
Tanya Shirazi

Managing Editor
Amanda Tien

Aster(ix) Contributing Editors
Rosa Alcalá, Arielle Greenberg, Yona Harvey, Daisy Hernandez, J. A. Howard, Sheila Maldonado, Dawn Lundy Martin, Oindrila Mukherjee, Idra Novey, Emily Raboteau, Nelly Rosario, Zohra Saed, Sun Yung Shin, Jenelle Troxell, Chika Unigwe, Marta Lucía Vargas, Autumn Womack, Elleni Centime Zeleke

Advisory Editors
Ari Ariel, Armando Garcia, Amy Sara Carroll, Norma Cantú, Xochi Candalaria, Jennifer Clement, Edwidge Danticat, Cristina García, Stephanie Elizondo Griest, Andrea Thome, Helena Maria Viramontes

Aster(ix) print issues are usually published twice a year with additional content online. **Aster(ix)** is funded in part by the Dietrich School of Arts and Sciences and the Department of English at University of Pittsburgh.

Aster(ix) Journal

presents

The Tarot Issue:

Chancletazo for Your Soul

by
Marlène Ramírez-Cancio

Edited by
Amanda Tien

December 2022

BLUE SKETCH PRESS | PITTSBURGH

ASTER(IX)—The Tarot Issue: Chancletazo for Your Soul. December 2022. Copyright © 2022 by Aster(ix) Journal and Marlène Ramírez-Cancio.

All rights reserved.

No part of this work may be reproduced, or stored in a retrieval system, or transmitted in any form or by any means, electronic, mechanical, photocopying, recording, or otherwise, without express written permission of the publisher, with the exception of educational institutions. Please write to Jesse Welch at 1 (one) 5th St., Pittsburgh, PA 15215 for information about permissions.

Individual acknowledgments available on pg. 67

Published via Blue Sketch Press, Pittsburgh.
www.bluesketchpress.com

The Tarot Issue: Chancletazo for Your Soul
December 2022
An Aster(ix) Anthology / Aster(ix) Journal
Edited by Amanda Tien—1st ed.

| ISBN (print) | 978-1-942547-19-8 (trade paperback) |
| | 1-942547-19-8 (ISBN-10) |

Cover art by Marlène Ramírez-Cancio
Cover Design by Little Owl Creative & Amanda Tien

First Edition: December 2022

Printed in the United States of America
9 8 7 6 5 4 3 2 1

Para Samara, mi sol,
y para Mami, mi árbol,
que ningún huracán tumba.

Contents

Introduction	12
The Major Arcana	**14**
0. El Chavo	14
I. El Walter	16
II. La Celia	18
III. La Momposina	20
IV. El Gabo	22
V. La Sor Juana	24
VI. Los Ocasio	26
VII. La Churro Lady	28
VIII. La Sylvia	30
IX. El Borges	32
X. El Huracán	34
XI. La Wise Latina	36
XII. La Cuarentena	38
XIII. El Acabose	40
XIV. La Piragua	42
XV. El Dictador	44
XVI. El Desmadre	46
XVII. La J.Lo	48
XVIII. La Sumac	50
XIX. La Nena	52
XX. La Epifanía	54
XXI. El Tan-Tán	56
A Conversation with the Artist & Writer, Marlène Ramírez-Cancio, and the Editor, Amanda Tien	59
Endnotes & Acknowledgments	67
About the Author & Aster(ix)	71

LA INTRODUCCIÓN

Somebody needed a nudge.

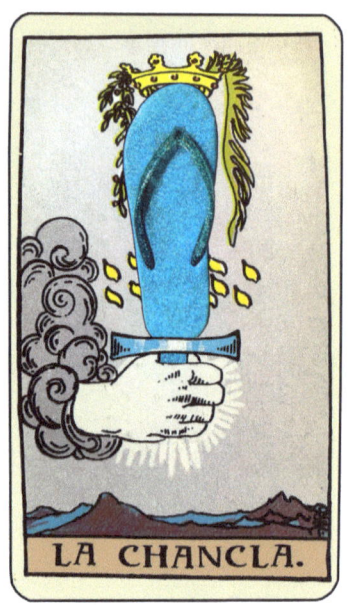

In May 2020, deep in the pandemic, Angie Cruz asked Marlène Ramírez-Cancio to do a tarot reading for someone who needed a push in the right direction. It was a gift, from one woman of color to another. Marlène joked the reading was a "chancletazo for the soul."

During tarot readings, Marlène found herself frequently referencing Latinx cultural icons and concepts when sharing the Major Arcana. So, for fun, she began to experiment with visual art by adding collage to the widely used 1909 Smith-Rider-Waite deck.

Angie soon introduced Marlène to Aster(ix)'s Managing Editor, Amanda Tien. Aster(ix) then established an Artist-in-Residence feature—for which Marlène was the inaugural resident artist. Amanda re-posted these cards on @asterixjournal every few weeks as Marlène made them from Fall 2020 onwards. In Fall 2022, Amanda suggested this special all-color issue to feature *Chancletazo for Your Soul* from start-to-finish.

We are proud and honored of the collaborative nature of this work. Aster(ix) exists to lift up others. We hope you enjoy–and don't forget to ask yourself The Big Questions.
Amanda & Angie

About this project
Chancletazo for Your Soul was born in practice, resulting in the following beautiful and powerful rendition of collage and words of the Major Arcana by Marlène Ramírez-Cancio. If you're interested in learning more about this project and the behind-the-scenes, please read the conversation between Marlène and Amanda at the end of this issue.

How to understand this deck
The *Chancletazo for Your Soul* Major Arcana is not a new version of the tarot—a deck of cards with associated meanings originating in Italian courts hundreds of years ago. Rather, this deck and book are meant to add a layer of new meaning to existing cards. For those of us who know these cultural and societal figures already, it adds enrichment to our understanding. For those who don't know them, we hope it adds a joyful new lens. This project features only the **Major Arcana**. When Major Arcana cards are pulled in a reading, participants are being asked to reflect on the big questions—the major, archetypal experiences—of our journey in this life. In these "strange and trying times," we all need a bit more of that, do we not?

We also want to note an approach to **reversals**, which is when a card is drawn upside-down. Marlène shares that reversals should be seen not as a bad omen or as the "opposite" of the card's meaning, but as useful signs: they are questions about what we are resisting, what we're afraid of, what's blocking us, or what we're not aligned with. Consider what you need to do to turn a card the right side up.

How to read this issue
You may enjoy reading this issue in order as a series of micro-essays and art, or you may refer to it in conjunction with your new or existing tarot practice. Whatever works for you, that's the choice.

0. EL CHAVO

¡TENÍA QUE SER EL CHAVO DEL OCHO!

Like **The Fool/El Loco** that inspires him, El Chavo sets out on his path with childlike abandon, looking up at the sky, smiling de par en par, carrying only what he needs in his tiny bundle, holding his beloved torta de jamón for nourishment.

If you get El Chavo in a reading, know that there is life beyond the wooden barrel, beyond the Bonita Vecindad. Where do you long to go? What do you hope to learn? Who do you need to become? Your journey has just begun.

Adjust your suspenders, open your stripy chest, and take this invitation to go forth, siempre palante, trusting your path. There's a whole world out there for you to be in community with.

El Chavo is life's way of cheering you on, hopping from foot to foot, and saying: "Eso! Eso! Eso!"

♪ "El Burrito" by Yerba Buena

If you didn't know... *"El Chavo del Ocho" was a long-running Mexican television sitcom about El Chavo, an eight year-old orphan in a tight-knit neighborhood. All the children were played by adults, including El Chavo, who wore a characteristic striped shirt and lived in a barrel.*

I. EL WALTER

FUEGO! TIERRA! AGUA! AIRE!

El Walter—like **The Magician/El Mago** he's always been—is here to remind you that you already have all the elements you need for your expansion and transformation. You got fire, you got earth, you got water, you got air—plus a special double-ended magic chancla wand, y de ñapita, a portal to infinity at your crown. El Walter knows you're not playing.

What are you going to do with this multidimensional power? What will you manifest?

Whatever it is, remember: You are magical, strong, wise; you're in touch with your intuition and able to translate it into action. Go ahead and wear your power like a fabulous cape. Be your divine self and shine with bejeweled sparkle.

And always—ya lo sabes—go through life con "mucho, mucho, mucho AMOR."

♫ "Unfunky UFO" by Parliament ("you got all that is really needed")

—

If you didn't know… Walter Mercado was a legendary Puerto Rican astrologer. He's featured here in one of his many capes, holding a chancla-tipped magic wand in his right hand.

II. LA CELIA

YOUR INNER BRUJA

If you are chosen by La Celia, bow down. Seriously, take a moment. Now feel your feet on the ground, your crown up above. A todopoderosa embodiment of **The High Priestess/La Sacerdotisa**, La Celia emerges from the depths to urge you to tap into your inner knowing, swim in your intuition, and channel your ancestral wisdom—using your energy as your emotional instrument. She is a healer, in touch with spirit, dreams, and the collective unconscious. She is the ocean, the ocean's mother, the glittery sea foam, the undercurrents. How are you diving into your own oceans?

If you get La Celia in a reading—especially if she comes up reversed—take it as a loving chancletazo to get in line with your inner bruja. Listen to Celia sing; if you hear "Yemaya Olodo" as "yema ya—o lodo" ("egg yolk now—or mud"), please hang up and try again. The world needs you with good reception.

♪ "Yemayá" by Celia Cruz

If you didn't know... *Celia Cruz was a Cuban singer known as the Queen of Salsa. Here, she sits in front of the Tree of Life, holding a scroll that reads "AZÚCAR" on the forward-facing side, referring to Celia's trademark shout (¡Azúcar!) during performances, and "LUCUMÍ" on the other, referring to the Yoruba religion Celia practiced.*

III. LA MOMPOSINA

AY YO LA SEMBRÉ...

If you've ever heard the earth-rooting voice of Totó La Momposina, you know you feel her canto in your deepest body. You're elevated by being grounded; you soar by feeling your roots. La Momposina—like **The Empress/La Emperatriz**—signals deep alignment with your body, with nature, with all acts of creation and receptivity.

If you get La Momposina in a reading, you're called to ground yourself in your most delicious self-expression, to dig your hands in your ever-renewing soil, to experience your sublime badassery. Like the verdolaga at her feet—¡por el suelo!—feel yourself expand and flower. Like the flame in her hand—¡la candela viva!—be guided by your burning passions, by what fires you up and arouses you to your core.

What is your most fertile creative power? How do you connect with your capacity for excellence? (Re)read Audre Lorde's "The Uses of the Erotic: The Erotic as Power." Consider the words of Puerto Rican poet Angelamaría Dávila, "¿Será que uno no entiende que deshojarse a diario no impide echar raíces?" ("Don't we understand that the daily of shedding our leaves won't prevent us from growing roots?")

♪ "La Verdolaga" & "La Candela Viva" by Totó La Momposina

If you didn't know... *Totó La Momposina is an Afro-Indigenous Colombian singer, pictured here with verdolaga/purslane at her feet.*

IV. EL GABO

MAKER OF WORLDS

"The world was so recent that many things lacked names, and in order to mention them you had to point." And just like that—¡el Boom!—Macondo was born in *One Hundred Years of Solitude*.

Like **The Emperor/El Emperador**, El Gabo is a consummate worldmaker and a widely-accepted leader. Not only does he create frameworks and universes of knowledge that define our (oh so magical) reality, he also represents power, authorship/authority, and a certain fatherly no-sé-qué.

If you get El Gabo in a reading, examine what systems organize your world. What rules do you follow or impose? What is your relationship to structure? Are you holding steady or are you giving away your power? Are your patriarchy alarms going off? Tranqui.

At his best, El Gabo is the steadfast yet fluid maestrx in you—your strong foundations, your ability to follow through, your powers of manifestation. What gorgeous worlds are you creating right now? (And can I come visit?)

♫ "Macondo" by Óscar Chávez

—

If you didn't know... Just like *The Empress/La Momposina*, Gabriel García Márquez is also a costeño from the Colombian Caribbean. He is crowned by a copy of *Cien Años de Soledad*. *Labels abound, inspired by Macando residents, including, lest they forget: "Dios existe" (God exists).*

V. LA SOR JUANA

"EL MUNDO ILUMINADO, Y YO DESPIERTA."

La Sor Juana—like **The Hierophant/El Sacerdote**—calls you to reflect on your deepest sources of faith. What are your spiritual beliefs, value systems, and ethical principles? How did those come into being for you? If you are guided by traditions, institutions, or doctrines, how do you integrate their teachings—or disidentify from them—and make them your own?

When you get La Sor Juana in a reading, it's time to examine the ways you make meaning in your life. What expired notions of yourself and your spirit can you revise? What are you yearning to learn next? It's a time of deep dives and—if you're open to it—life-changing revelations. Self-taught from a very young age, Sor Juana Inés de la Cruz became a prolific author and protofeminist, satirized the patriarchy, and was openly in love with a woman—all from within the confines of a Catholic convent in 17th-century Mexico.

Call on your inner Juana to examine your deep-held beliefs—and trust yourself, casting off the "qué dirán."

♪ "Corrido de Sor Juana" by Astrid Hadad

If you didn't know... *Sor Juana Inés de la Cruz was a 17th-Century Mexican author and nun. A key in the shape of a female sign floats at her skirts. Kneeling behind her, two balding men; the letters "H" and "N" on their heads stand for "Hombres Necios" (Foolish Men).*

VI. LOS OCASIO

WONDER OCASIO POWERS, ACTIVATE!
FORM OF… A FLUID BUNNY! SHAPE OF… ABOLISH ICE!

Often misunderstood, Los Ocasio—like **The Lovers/Los Enamorados**—isn't a unidimensional card of romantic love. Are Alexandria Ocasio Cortez (AOC) and Benito Martínez Ocasio (Bad Bunny) lovers? That would be hot, but no. They share a last name, an island of origin, and, in their own arenas, they're passionate in their commitment to cultural transformation toward political change.

The utter fuckyessery of this card (also known as "The Decision") lies in making a choice from a place of individual power while trusting the "we," merging forces, and leading with mucho, mucho amor (thus El Walter up above as an angel). If you get Los Ocasio in a reading, ask yourself: Is this a big unconditional YES for me? Am I making this decision without reservation, de todo corazón?

If the energy of Los Ocasio beckons, your effusive outpouring of love (for a project, for a movement, for other humans) will likely result in a sea change. Check in with yourself, perrea sola o acompañada, and once you feel the YES, bump those lightning-sparking fists and—activate!

♪ "Estamos Bien" by Bad Bunny

If you didn't know… *Alexandria Ocasio Cortez (AOC) is a U.S. Congress Representative (D-NY) and activist. Bad Bunny is a rapper and singer. Purple is the color of royalty, and also, the Wonder Twins.*

VII. LA CHURRO LADY

¡ECHAPALANTE, PUES!

La Churro Lady, like the warrior in **The Chariot/El Carro**, is a courageous guerrera who stands her ground, knows her worth, and is determined to succeed—even as outside forces and systems of oppression try to block her. She won't let anything get in the way of her carrito, which brings priceless energy to weary travelers.

If you get La Churro Lady in a reading, you're being called to assert your independence, have fierce grit, and move toward your goal with sweetness-fueled confidence. This is a card of encouragement, conviction and ganas. How can you stand your ground? And at the same time, what pushes you forward? La Churro Lady is the last card of the first line of the Major Arcana—she urges you to go forth y no echar patrás ni pa tomar impulso.

You're in the first phase of your journey—you're sure to move on to bigger and greater platforms—but with La Churro Lady in your corner, you're poised to hold your head up high as you push forward and show your value to the world.

♪ "¡Echapalante!" by Jarana Beat

If you didn't know... *1) Churros are delicious fried pastries coated in cinnamon sugar. You should get one. Actually, we should go get one, too. 2) Although the woman in this image is Spanish churro chef Rosario Salguero Venegas, "Charo la de los Churros," this card was actually inspired by Elsa, the NYC "Churro Lady" who stood her ground against cops who used unnecessary force to remove her and her cart in November 2019. See our endnotes for more info.*

VIII. LA SYLVIA

"I'M NOT MISSING A MINUTE OF THIS. IT'S THE REVOLUTION!"

A powerful symbol of **Strength/La Fuerza**, La Sylvia is in full command of her inner lion. Unafraid to roar to confront the world, she embodies courage, passion, and unshakeable resolve. Like El Walter, La Sylvia has an eternity symbol above her head, signaling her access to eternal source; the star is her mark of dignity and justice.

If you get La Sylvia in a reading, you're being called to step into your power. Your revolution is finally here! Are you ready? Feel the fire in your belly and remember you are strong, no matter who's with you and who's not. You've been here before, you persevered, and you'll do it again. Are people saying you're "too much," "too loud," or "too forceful"? Pafuera! Stay committed to your cause. Guide yourself and others with your primordial strength, fighting for what's right.

Y que La Sylvia te acompañe.

🎵 "Queen of This Shit" by Quay Dash

If you didn't know... *Sylvia Rivera was a Puerto Rican and Venezuelan trans activist. She worked with Marsha P. Johnson (who you can see on the button pinned to her dress), an American trans liberation activist, on a radical political collective, Street Transvestite Action Revolutionaries (STAR). The sign features the symbol and call-to-action of STAR.*

IX. EL BORGES

YOU, YOURSELF, AND TÚ

What is your relationship to stillness? To soledad? Like **The Hermit/ El Ermitaño**, El Borges is a card of cultivating solitude in search of knowledge. You may at times feel blind like Borges, but like him, you carry wisdom in your own lamp—that point of illumination from which you can see everything that ever was and ever will be.

If you get El Borges in a reading, take it as a strong invitation to turn off your devices, pause your search for external validation, and turn to yourself as your biggest resource. What gems are in your inner library? What sacred knowledge?

This is a time to meditate, reflect, study, write in your notebook, look back at the year you've had, recognize what you've already learned and contemplate what might come next. This is not about abject isolation and loneliness, but about soledad (for which, as Tato Laviera wrote, "there is no English translation.") Turn to yourself as a sage, get clarity on what you want, who you are, where you're going, and light your own camino to get there.

♪ "Road to Self" by Aisha Badru

If you didn't know… *Jorge Luis Borges was an Argentine writer. He's dressed in gray, a color Borges associates with immortality and wisdom. His lamp contains El Aleph—the first letter in the Hebrew alphabet and the title of one of his short stories.*

X. EL HURACÁN

"SANTA MARÍA, LÍBRANOS DE TODO MAL…"

Few things say "cycle" like a spinning cyclone. El Huracán, like the karmic twists of fate in **The Wheel of Fortune/La Rueda de la Fortuna**, reminds us there are cyclical forces at play that are completely out of our control.

If you get El Huracán in a reading, you're being called to accept that what you're going through—whether it be a challenging phase or a wonderful one—may hinge on something that is not up to you. What you can control is how you choose to respond. Do you throw paper towels at a flooded city? Or do you rise to the moment and lead with grace? Do you hoard supplies and lock yourself at home with your power generator? Or do you share your habichuelas with your neighbors?

El Huracán invites you to be fully in the present and remember that what goes around, comes around.

🎵 "Santa María," traditional Puerto Rican plena (and "It's Not Up to You" by Björk)

If you didn't know… *Hurricane Maria, pictured here from a satellite, devastated Puerto Rico in 2017. The islands lost electricity, water, and gasoline. The red devil with an un-presidented hairstyle drops paper towels, a meager offering to people like my mother, whose house was completely destroyed by the storm.*

XI. LA WISE LATINA

CHECK YOURSELF!

La Wise Latina reigns supreme, holding the proverbial scales of **Justice/La Justicia** in one hand and, in the other, a sharp sword pointing straight up to the heavens—she's made a decisively fair, clear, and logical ruling. With the richness of her experiences, she can understand the difficult choices you've had to make; she'll bring her whole self to bear in her deliberations, reaching a better conclusion than others who have not lived that life.

If you get La Wise Latina in a reading, ask yourself: Am I acting ethically and with integrity, valuing the truth, and looking out for the greater good of all concerned? You'd better hope so, because otherwise she'll hit you with a dissent so fierce, you'll be feeling her chancletazo for weeks and months to come.

She's holding down the fort, fighting foolishness left and right, so please work with her, gente. And if others have acted unfairly toward you… ay bendito. This tía WILL hold them accountable. Punto final.

♫ "A Wise Latina" by Arturo O'Farrill & the Afro Jazz Orchestra

---

If you didn't know… *Sonia Sotomayor is the first woman of color, first Hispanic, and first Latina to serve as a U.S. Supreme Court Justice. She assumed office in August 2008.*

XII. LA CUARENTENA

RESPIRA.

Like **The Hanged Man/El Colgado**, La Cuarentena indicates a time of forced repose. You may not be experiencing an actual quarantine, but life has hit the pause button; no matter how trapped you feel, there's little choice but to surrender to the lull.

If you get La Cuarentena in a reading, you are called to accept an uncomfortable—but possibly transformative—moment of suspension. While everything seems to be upside down, ask yourself: What new ways of seeing become available to me from this position? Is there a life-altering perspective for me to discover? What are the lessons of slowing down?

After a near-fatal bus accident, Frida Kahlo was "bored as hell in bed with a plaster cast" (her words) and started painting for the first time. She had a mirror installed above her bed and used a special easel to paint while lying down—thus began her inimitable self-portraits and her life as an artist.

Hang on, look around, and allow La Cuarentena to be a time of enlightenment.

🎵 "SOS - Interlude" by Natalia Doco

If you didn't know… Frida Kahlo is a self-taught Mexican painter who is most famous for her self-portraits from the 1930s and 40s. I started this project, **Chancletazo for Your Soul***, during the early months of The Quarantine in the Covid Pandemic. Frida is pictured here wearing a white face mask along with the spider monkey keeping her company.*

XIII. EL ACABOSE

AND—SCENE.

El Acabose—**like Death/La Muert**e—is the great letting go, el gran kaput. As La Lupe belted out in 1969: "Se acabóoo, lo nuestro está muertooo." (She then kindly translates: "Se acabó in English means: it's over, baby, all over!") If you get El Acabose in a reading, it's a sign that something must end. Pum, cayó la piedra. Zapepallá. Yes, El Acabose can clear the way for new and awe-inspiring things in your life, but first you must accept this ending.

What do you know, deep down, you need to release? What has outlived its purpose? What old stories, stale beliefs, or untenable situations must you obliterate? This may be a painful time for you—or it may be a time of relief. Either way, know that there's no use holding on any longer.

Cry if you have to, play torch songs at full volume, let your eyeliner stream down your face, telenovela-style—do what you need to do, but don't be in denial.

It's time for you to let go. Only then will you be ready for new beginnings, open to embracing fresh energies that can transform you. Yo voy a ti.

🎵 "Se Acabó" by La Lupe

If you didn't know... *La Lupe was a Cuban singer. Her energetic performances are captured here with a laughing face that's also crying (don't we all know that feeling?).*

XIV. LA PIRAGUA

CÓGELO CON TEIQUIRISI…

Like **Temperance/La Templanza**, La Piragua is a card of balance, flow, and alchemy, in which seemingly disparate elements come together to bring about the perfect harmony. A piragua, in Puerto Rico, is the delightful snow cone that helps us cool down in the Caribbean heat, while in Colombia, a piragua is a wooden canoe that flows down rivers and inspires classic cumbias.

If you get La Piragua in a reading, cool down and flow. This card invokes both water and earth for you—the canoe sits partly in the water and partly on the ground, and the piragua combines frozen water with the incomparable fruits of the earth. This means it's time to dive into your intuition while also leaning into your practical, grounded self, trusting the balance between the two.

What situations require your patience right now? What combination of elements can you call upon to achieve—and maintain—your equilibrium? Meditate, imagining you're in a sturdy canoe, floating placidly on calm waters…while a cool frambuesa syrup flows from the top of your head all the way down your spine. Mmmmm. Breathe in, hum a little cumbia, and smile.

♫ "La Piragua" by José Barros, as performed by Gabriel Romero

---

If you didn't know… *The face here is José Barros, the indigenous Colombian composer of "La Piragua." On his chest, the icon of a piragua cone features the reiki symbol Nin Giz Zida for calming and grounding.*

XV. EL DICTADOR

TIME TO LOOK IN THE MIRROR.

El Dictador, like **The Devil/El Diablo**, is a stop-everything signal for you to face your shadow self. You know the one. Your jealous, insecure, self-sabotaging, cruel, addicted, vindictive inner tyrant. As the dark side of El Walter, El Dictador uses its power not to generate love for self and others, but to dominate, torture, and annihilate. It's that sharp-toothed gremlin that jumps out of nowhere, wreaks havoc, and—if you're lucky and self-aware—leaves you with that "tierra trágame" swamp-pit in your stomach.

If you get El Dictador in a reading, don't panic. Face the low-key Pinochet you tend to ignore in yourself, and get curious: What is this behavior costing you? Where is all that shame and anger lodged in your body? And what practices will help you subvert this internal oppressor?

It's not pretty, and you might have to make amends, but if you call upon your powers of manifestación (bilingual double-pow!), you and the world will be all the better for it. We've all been there. Be kind to yourself.

♪ "Rising" by Lhasa De Sela

If you didn't know... *The Devil—who has an oval mirror for a face—wears the familiar gray hat and cape of Chilean dictator Augusto Pinochet. The two figures below him, who are naked and chained, also have mirrors as faces. Between them, a gremlin.*

XVI. EL DESMADRE

¡AY MAMÁ!

El Desmadre—like the oft-dreaded **The Tower/La Torre**—signals a big ontological earthquake, a time when your very foundations are being shaken, your roots pulled out from under you. In Spanish, a "desmadre" is not just any chaos, it is the mother of all chaos—a disorder so profound, it's as if all our mothers suddenly disappeared and everything fell apart. It is, quite literally, a "dis-mothering."

If you get El Desmadre in a reading, it signals a time of profound structural change. It might feel like you're losing all your familiar ground. But take heart: this is more likely—especially after the reckoning of El Dictador—a crumbling of old structures, stories, relationships, or identities that have been trapping you in a tower, not letting you grow.

The comforting ay-bendito mother might not be here, but El Desmadre is the most radical chancletazo. 'Approvechate' this moment, take stock, and—when the time comes—rebuild from the ground up.

♪ "When It Comes Down" by Spiritchild

If you didn't know… Those two human figures have the face of my mother! That crown labeled "MAMÁ" is dislodged from the tower, and they fall amongst blue flip-flop chanclas.

XVII LA J.LO

DESPUÉS DEL DESMADRE, LA ESTRELLA

La J.Lo—**like The Star/La Estrella**—signals a time of radiance, good fortune, and effortless feelings of confidence. Perched majestically at the edge of a pond, her feet in the water with her heels still touching the earth, La J.Lo pours out her sparkly potion into the waters of unfuckwithability. (Or maybe it's the Fountain of Youth, quién sabe.) The seven stars in the sky represent the chakras, illuminated from within and connected to self.

If you get this card in a reading, it means your "J.Lo Effect" is in full force. Relish it! You're in a period of reality-defying magnificence. Be fearless. Take leaps.

Not only are you in touch with your superstar superpowers, but the external world is also smiling on you, abriendo caminos, conspiring to protect you and your delicious dreams. Listen to your inner voice as it sings through your whole body. Befriend the crowned birds, the tips of mountains, the giggling rivers.

"Live your life and stay young"—La J.Lo's got (your) back.

♫ "Algo Está Cambiando" by Bomba Estéreo (& your favorite J.Lo song)

If you didn't know... *Jennifer Lopez is a Nuyorican superstar. (Have you really not heard of J.Lo?)*

XVIII. LA SUMAC

SIT WITH YOUR MIEDO

With her uncanny voice like a human theremin, La Sumac —like **The Moon/La Luna**— is here to ask: What are you afraid of? What are your dreams telling you? What's keeping you up at night? La Sumac is a dual card speaking to your depths—the depths of anxiety and fear, but also the depths of your intuition and embodied knowing.

If you get this card in a reading, ask yourself: What messages is my subconscious trying so desperately to give me? Listen with your whole body. Let the thinking mind take a break. What rituals, what symbols, what brujería is required of you at this time? What is the black cat on the left trying to tell you?

Allow the moon flowers to open and glow in the dark, lighting a path ahead. Listen to the full range of your intuitive voices, from the high-pitched glass-shatterers to the lowest of the bone voices. Vibrate with them, embrace the unease, liberate the coded messages. It's all there for you to uncover, under the moonlight, if you can sit with your miedo and listen for answers.

♪ "Ataypura!" by Yma Sumac

If you didn't know... Yma Sumac was a Peruvian-American singer. The lobster has teeth as pincers; in dream psychology, losing teeth in dreams is a symbol of fear of loss and important life changes. And who isn't afraid of getting stuck in an elevator?

XIX. LA NENA

¡AY MI NENA LINDA, MI SOL!

When was your last carcajada?

La Nena—like **The Sun/El Sol**—is a card of joy, freedom, optimism, and réquete-superabundant fun. If your inner kid wants to ride a pink unicorn through a field of sunflowers, they can do that! If you get La Nena in a reading, it means it's time to shine, to play, to revel in life's pleasures. There's an irresistibly youthful energy in this card that can make you feel rejuvenated, tickled into brightness.

As you take in this Leo fire, let yourself do what makes you feel exuberant. What areas of your life do you want to take dancing under the sunlight? Where is your creativity bubbling up? Focus on those life-giving energies as you laugh with La Nena during this time of unabashed optimism. Go out to see and be seen, be generous. Be the light.

This is you in all your gorgeousness, amorcito! Enjoy it!

🎵 "La Nena" by Milena Warthon

If you didn't know... *this is the face of my 8-year-old daughter, used with her consent.*

XX. LA EPIFANÍA

RING , RING!

What's that sound? Oh! It's the Universe calling—and you're answering the call.

La Epifanía, like **Judgment/El Juicio**, is here to announce that you're leveling up, rising from the dead (and the dead ends), and following your sacred calling. It's an awakening, an epiphany, a Life Purpose download from your all-star best selves. Descarga!

If you get La Epifanía in a reading, take it as an endorsement from the heavens, a sign that you're moving in the right direction. You're in alignment with your highest values. You're this close to a major breakthrough. And you probably have a posse. As playwright Paula Vogel has said, "circles rise together"—so choose your people wisely and make sure you uplift one another during this momentous time.

When I say "your sacred calling," what's the first thing you see yourself doing? Are you doing it? La Epifanía says: Do it now.

♪ "Voy a Vivir para Siempre" by Fania All-Stars

If you didn't know… *the Fania All-Stars are a group formed in 1968 in New York City to showcase musicians from Fania, the leading salsa record label of the time. Pictured left to right: Cheo Feliciano, Héctor Lavoe, Johnny Pacheco (Fania founder), Puerto Rican trombone player Willie Colón at center, Celia Cruz, Ray Barretto, and Rubén Blades. The design of the title, La Epifanía, evokes the Fania All Stars logo.*

XXI. EL TAN-TÁN

ÚLTIMA PARADA: RANCHERA

How do Ranchera songs end? Two notes: "Tan-tán"! The satisfying sound of completion.

Like The World/El Mundo, El Tan-Tán announces your triumphant arrival at the finish line. You made it! If you get El Tan-Tán in a reading, consider it the ultimate mic drop. You did a thing, and you're on top of the world, carajo!

At the beginning of this journey, El Walter encouraged you with the four elements and a magic chancla wand. Here, here Lola Beltrán holds two double-chancla wands, plus the combined gritos of her four compañeras. AJÚA! Are you feeling the collective power? How will you celebrate your accomplishment? What song will you blast? Consider Lola's last line in "La Chancla," as she belts out: "¡Que la chancla que yo tiro / No la vuelvo a levantar!"

Nuff said.

 "La Chancla," as sung by Lola Beltrán

If you didn't know… the *"tan-tán"* are the two notes, often a down-up sound, played at the end of ranchera songs. Ranchera is a genre of traditional music in Mexico dating before the 1900s that is still played regionally today. Mexican musicians like Amalia Mendoza, Lucha Reyes, Lucha Villa, and Chavela Vargas inspire from the four corners. At the center is Lola Beltrán who is known as one of Mexico's most acclaimed singers of Ranchera and Huapango music.

LA CONVERSACIÓN

Amanda Tien (AJT), issue editor: You did it! You've been making this project for close to two years!

Marlène Ramírez-Cancio (MRC), artist and author: *We* did it! I really do feel that. If I didn't have the container of the Aster(ix) artist residency, and especially the loving support from you and [Aster(ix) Editor-in-Chief] Angie Cruz, I never would have finished Chancletazo for Your Soul, punto. This work was and is collaborative.

AJT: Tarot was first invented in Italian courts in the 15th century, and has evolved with usage and meaning. Today, many people use tarot as a way of constructive conversation, a kind of therapy. The cards then become helpful visual reminders to distill big ideas and complicated situations. How did you start to become involved with tarot and doing readings for people?

MRC: I can't remember the exact moment I first picked up tarot cards, but I saw from old diaries that I was reading them for myself in college. In the early pandemic, I did a reading on Zoom for Angie, and then she wanted to have me do one for a friend. Mujer Que Pregunta (my tarot and Process Doula practice) began as a gift from one woman of color to another. Readings are a very intimate experience, and because it was a time when it was impossible to be together in person, we had to find other ways to connect. People allowed themselves to be more vulnerable, I think. Many of my readings were for artists whose livelihoods had been upended by the pandemic, so they were very big questions to explore. How do I survive? What do I really want? What should I do next? What opportunities does this give me?

AJT: Angie gifted me a tarot reading session with you when I started officially as Aster(ix) Managing Editor because she knew I was feeling worried about finishing my first novel. My conversation with you crystalized and named so many things. I still have the cards you pulled for me pinned up by my desk. You are really, really good at doing readings. It was one of the most singularly effective and beautiful conversations I've ever had. So, first, thank you, again. And two, what is the experience like for you on the other side?

MRC: I so appreciate you sharing that with me. I've learned something surprising about myself as I've done more of these. I get very invested in those one-hour conversations. I even get goosebumps when I hear someone say something that is clearly so very true for them, something that perhaps they are just realizing aloud for the first time. I find myself being so in it, so attuned to their little moments. But afterwards—it's weird—I forget what was said. I wouldn't have believed it. It's like I channel things in the moment of hyper-intense connection. But if I didn't take photos of the readings or follow up with notes, whatever I said during a session would just disappear. My mind just puts it away.

So I'm really grateful to you for the chance to memorialize this project and this process so I don't forget it, haha! I keep coming back to the hashtag #ThePandemicMadeMeDoIt which I used to add at the end of my instagram posts, because Chancletazo For Your Soul really maps my own Fool's journey—my own El Chavo journey—through the pandemic, from one job to another, one life stage to another.

AJT: I think that's why we were so excited to have La Cuarentena as the cover of the issue, too, yes?

MRC: Yes! The Hanged Man Card came up often in my readings over the last few years–I started calling it the Pandemic Card.

AJT: I got that one too!

MRC: Aha, yes! It's a forced repose, a forced pause from which new illumination and perspective can come. So that cover I think felt like a natural choice to both of us for so many reasons.

For me, on the other side of tarot readings, there's a lot of love. It's sincere love for others and what they're going through as people. This hardcore cheerleading Process Doula conversation with pretty tarot pictures condensed into one hour. It's beautiful. I get so much out of it, I learn so much.

AJT: Like what?

MRC: I learn from the things that repeat. They repeat in two different ways: 1) How cards repeat for the same person, and how the deck seems to be almost yelling at them across time and space that they bring up the same cards over and over, saying hey! pay attention! and 2) the repetition of issues from person to person. I can tell you, for example, that almost everyone has said something about Impostor Syndrome. Everyone thinks it's them. They say, "I am not…, why am I not…" and I want to say, "Que no panda el cúnico [don't panic], que pretty much everyone is feeling that!" I'm not a therapist, but reading tarot has really given me an appreciation for how we're all connected and how we all have childhood trauma, unresolved issues, and secret dreams, and how these things keep affecting us as grown people—especially as women/femmes of color. We just need reminders sometimes. Mujer Que Pregunta comes from a phrase in Spanish that means, "A woman who asks is a woman who (already) knows." So even you keeping those cards up on your wall—they're reminders; you already have those answers within you.

AJT: Ooh, which brings me to the title of the project. Can you share about that?

MRC: Yes! So, a chancletazo refers to the way that Latina moms or grandmas would spank your butt with a flip-flop (a chancleta or chancla) to get you to pay attention or to scold you. It's an iconic cultural reference, and the subject of much retrospective humor. Por cierto: I've struggled with the violent implications of the title, because, who really wants to endorse a spanking? Not me. I mean it as a loving nudge, a call to attention, paying homage to the rubber chancla. And then a Zen practitioner told me about the concept of the "Zen slap," startling you into shape, into recognizing something, into awakening you to something. And to me that's the same thing. Y mira—if a slap can be Zen, then I can have my chancletazo and laugh about it too.

In practice, the concept came to me when I pulled reversed cards for people during readings, like say, an upside down Empress or Sun. I'd ask them, "What kind of chancletazo"—and I'd tap the card with my finger to rotate it—"do you need to turn this card right side up?" The question always made people laugh, then get quiet and think. I see this nudge as a way to help people be most attuned and empowered by their ideals. It's not meant to sting, it's not meant to hurt. It's meant to align you to yourself. And it's meant to be a little funny. I've done a lot of satire and parody, so there's elements of that here too. If you think of that book *Chicken Soup for Your Soul*, and see *Chancletazo for Your Soul* as an abuela-style take on self-help... Ves? La Chancla can heal! Also, it seems to be memorable, because I've gotten calls from people saying, "Marlène, I was just sitting here obsessing and I need one of your chancletazos." So it seems useful as an action-image.

AJT: You've shared with me before that you sometimes felt like you were just making it up as you went along. I know you taught yourself Photoshop doing this project. When did you start to get that confidence?

MRC: Confidence or carifresquería? Ha! I was always a literature person, and then some years ago a psychic said to me I was a "visual artist." And I was like yeah right, you're way off, lady. And when this project started to go really well, I remember Angie called me and said, "See, I told you the psychic was right!" There was a moment after the first six or seven cards that just sort of clicked for me. And it's made me think, who's to say that you're not "that" kind of artist? Don't let anyone (even yourself) say, "Oh, you're only allowed to be a visual artist" or "only a fiction writer," or whatever. Who made you believe that? (That's me talking to myself.) I even noticed that a lot of my cards included musicians and were accompanied by songs that were important to me; I really have zero musical knowledge or skill, but yet, musical references came to me. This process was getting myself where I was never meant to be, and finding my place in it—while having fun.

AJT: At the beginning of remaking the Major Arcana, you were specifically creating the collages to share on Instagram. How did creating for social media shape your process?

MRC: I was reading for people and I noticed I kept referencing certain icons from my childhood (like el Chavo del Ocho or Walter Mercado), and so I wanted to share those added layers to share with others. I had been doing readings on Zoom, so I was already doing that work in the digital realm at a distance, and Instagram felt sort of a natural platform to extend the work. El Chavo was the first one, because he carries the same bundle The Fool does—so it was an add-on to reference when explaining The Fool to a Latinx person.

The audience on Instagram that I conjured in my mind was bilingual, so I wrote my captions with some Espanglish, and it was a joyful process. Writing visual descriptions also forced me to reckon with what images were included in the card and why. So the process of writing the visual descriptions became part of writing the text in general. And knowing that people could search for songs immediately and play them lent it this multisensorial experience that I was feeling in myself. It had a visual element, a written element, and then the audio, and it was a way to play and share that multitude. You did a great job leading the way on converting those visual descriptions to the If you didn't know… sections. And OMAIGÁ! The research you did around the images I took off the internet? Amazing. Thank you, Amanda. I'm your forever fan.

AJT: I learned so much making those! Thank you for sharing. You are a joy to work with, and I think this kind of work—guided reflections, encouragement, something beautiful, making something out of pieces, and of course the power of tarot to make us think—is exciting. You told me that El Chavo and El Walter came really naturally to you. We've been working on the Instagram collaboration of this project going on two years (wow!), and I know that some cards weren't so easy.

MRC: There were some icons and cultural figures I thought about including in this project, and it was hard to narrow it down! And you know this better than anyone, but it took me a year to get the final two, Judgment and The World. In the Major Arcana, they indicate coming to a place of completion, the end of the hero's/Fool's journey. It's really big emotions, concepts, and I had no idea what in the hell I was going to use for those epic cards. I talked to a LOT of people about it, and bless them for brainstorming with me. Pero in the end, La Epifanía and El Tan-Tán revealed themselves to me while I was resting, lying on my bed doing "nothing," and they appeared right as the deadline was approaching (how convenient, ha!).

El Tan-Tán is the last card I figured out, but ironically, it has always been with me. Many years ago, in twentieth-century San Francisco, as part of the Latina Theatre Lab collective I was in a show called Last Stop Ranchera. My friend Monica Sánchez, who is an incredible writer and performer, wrote this beautiful opening piece about seeking the genesis of the ubiquitous tan-tán, exploring the question: why do rancheras end with tan-tán? She tracked it to the beating of the heart: Tan-tán, tan-tán, tan-tán. And I have lived with this tan-tán in my own heart ever since. It was like it was the deepest, most ancient card within me in the whole deck, and yet it was the one that was least visible to me as I searched for it. And when I stopped searching for it, it was right there! It was the only possibility for the card of completion, for the ultimate mic drop. And what I like about it is that, yes, while it indicates the end of a song, it means that another song can begin. Like this project, this phase might be over, but now it's time for the next. It's an incredibly fulfilling moment. And now we can begin another journey.

el fin

Endnotes & Acknowledgments

This issue features collage with the Smith-Rider-Waithe tarot deck and images found from the internet and made into new collages (for example, the "image" of Jennifer Lopez on card XVII does not exist in reality – it is a heavy conglomeration of many elements). We have attempted to list attributions when possible for the most notable of the original images below, and we are grateful to be a space to feature the power of collage. We believe this work is protected under the Fair Use Act for the purposes of commentary, criticism, and scholarship. This literary journal is a not-for-profit artistic endeavor to highlight and lift up the creative work of BIPOC womxn from around the world.

Selected Image Attributions

The **deck** is inspired, shaped, and built upon the base tarot card design by **Pamela Colman Smith** which were first published in Rider-Waite-Smith deck in 1909. Smith's designs were influenced by the 19th-century magician and occultist Eliphas Levi, as well as by the teachings of the Hermetic Order of the Golden Dawn.

O. El Chavo features a screenshot from the television show El Chavo del Ocho (1973–1975, Canal 8, starring and created by Roberto Gómez Bolaños, aka Chespirito.)

I. El Walter features a photo of Walter Mercado by Harry Langdon via Getty Images.

II. La Celia features a black-and-white headshot of Celia Cruz by Herrera Studios, shared by Omer Pardillo-Cid.

III. La Momposina features a photo of Totó la Momposina by Josh Pulman.

IV. El Gabo features a photo of Gabriel García Márquez by Isabel Steva Hernandez/Colita/Corbis/Flickr.

V. La Sor Juana features a portrait of Sor Juana Inés de la Cruz by Miguel Cabrera painted in the early 1700s.

VI. Los Ocasio features a headshot of AOC by Collier Schorr for TIME, and one of Bad Bunny by Isaac Brekken/Getty Images.

VII. La Churro Lady features a photo taken in 2014 by Sharon Minkoff of a churro maker Rosario Salguero Venegas, nicknamed Charo "la de los churros," in El Puerto de Santa María, Spain. The text refers to a November 2019 incident where a churro seller named Elsa was forcibly arrested in New York City. Read the articles below for more info:

    Paybarah, Azi. "Police Face a Backlash After Woman Selling Churros Is Handcuffed." New York Times, 11 Nov. 2019, www.nytimes.com/2019/11/11/nyregion/churro-lady-Subway-arrest.html.

    Rivoli, Dan. "Viral Video of Churro Lady in Cuffs Sparks Protest Against MTA's Police Plan." Spectrum News NY1, 12 Nov. 2019, www.ny1.com/nyc/all-boroughs/news/2019/11/12/viral-video-of-churro-lady-in-cuffs-sparks-protest-against-mta-s-police-plan.

VIII. La Sylvia features a photo of Sylvia Rivera taken in 1996 by Valerie Shaff.

IX. El Borges features a photo of Jorge Luis Borges in Palermo, Sicily taken in 1984 by Levan Ramishvili, shared on Flickr.

X. El Huracán features a National Oceanic and Atmospheric Administration (NOAA) satellite infrared image of Hurricane Maria making landfall near Yabucoa, Puerto Rico on September 20, 2017.

XI. La Wise Latina features a portrait of the Honorable Sonia Sotomayor taken by Elena Seibert.

XII. La Cuarentena features Frida Kahlo's Self Portrait 1940 II, and a spider monkey from Getty Images.

XIII. El Acabose features the cover art of an album by La Lupe, Lupe Victoria Yolí Raymond. We believe the correct attribution is the art design by Michael Forman in 1974 for Tico Records, LO MEJOR DE LA LUPE, FACD 1318.

XIV. La Piragua features a smiling photograph of the composer José Barros we believe was taken by his son, John Barros, who shared it in an August 14, 2019 retrospective called "ESPECIAL | Cinco décadas de 'La Piragua'" at semanarural.com.

XV. El Dictador features a photo (with the face cropped out) of Augusto Pinochet by Cris Bouroncle forAFP/Getty, and a gremlin from the

1984 black comedy film, Gremlins.

XVI. El Desmadre features photos I took of my mother in 2021.

XVII. La J.Lo features a conglomeration of photographs of Jennifer Lopez attributed to Getty from her October 2014 "We Can Survive" concert.

XVIII. La Sumac features a photo of Yma Sumac in the 1950s from the Michael Ochs Archives via Getty Images.

XIX. La Nena features an image of my daughter from 2022.

XX. La Epifanía features photos of some members of the Fania All-Stars. We had difficulty finding attribution for all of the photos. The photo of Johnny Pacheco is by Craft Recordings. We believe the following photos were promotional from Fania (and cannot find photographer attributions): Celia Cruz, Willie Colón, Ray Barretto (from the cover of his 1973 album Indestructible), and Rubén Blades.

XXI. El Tan-Tán features a photo of Chavela Vargas taken by Pedro Valtierra and held by the Archivo/CUARTOSCURO. We could not find photographer attributions for three album covers: the photo of Lucha Reyes is from a 1964 album by RCA Victor, Lo Mejor de Lucha Reyes; the photo Lucha Villa is from her 1974 album by Musarts, Lucha Villa; and the photo of Amalia Mendoza is from her 1958 album with RCA Victor, La Tariácuri. We believe the portrait of Lola Beltrán was taken by her cinema studio for promotion for one of the dozens of films she starred in during the 1950s and 1960s.

About the Artist-Author

Marlène Ramírez-Cancio (2021-22 Aster(ix) Artist in Residence) is a Puerto Rican cultural producer, artist, and educator based in Lenapehoking, aka Brooklyn. She is the Founding Director of EmergeNYC, an incubator and network for emerging artists-activists in NYC and beyond, focused on developing the artistic expression of people of color and LGBTQAI+ folks. In 2021, she brought the incubator to BAX/Brooklyn Arts Exchange, where she is currently Director of EmergeNYC and Practice Lab. Through Mujer Que Pregunta, Marlène works as a tarot practitioner and Process Doula to help BIPOC cultural workers shape their ideas, clarify their purpose, and make sure their projects align with the goals of their practice. When the dinosaurios roamed the Earth, she co-founded Fulana, a Latina satire collective whose videos have been shown internationally at film festivals, museums, and universities. Marlène serves on the Steering Committee of LxNY/Latinx Arts Consortium of New York, the Board of Directors of the National Performance Network, and the Board of Advisors of The Action Lab and the Center for Artistic Activism. She is the mom of a wonderful child, and is currently learning how to sew her own clothes. | **mujerquepregunta.com**

To keep exploring...

See more of The Tarot Issue (including listening to a Spotify playlist of all the songs listed!) and to other work published by Aster(ix), please visit **www.asterixjorunal.com**, scan the QR code, or follow Aster(ix) on Instagram, Twitter, and Facebook at @asterixjournal

www.ingramcontent.com/pod-product-compliance
Lightning Source LLC
Chambersburg PA
CBHW040203100526
44592CB00006B/90